SEALS

Written and edited by **Lucy Baker**

Consultant Sea Mammal Research Unit,
British Antarctic Survey

Kids Can Press

Kids Can Press Ltd
TORONTO

CANADIAN CATALOGUING IN PUBLICATION DATA

Baker, Lucy
Seals

ISBN 0-921103-81-6

1. Seals (Animals) – Juvenile literature. 2. Creative activities and seat work –
Juvenile literature. 3. Games – Juvenile literature. I. Title.

QL737. P6B3 1990 j599.74'8 C89-095099-7

Kids Can Press Ltd
585½ Bloor Street West
Toronto, Ontario, Canada M6G 1K5

First published in Great Britain by
Two-Can Publishing Ltd
27 Cowper Street
London EC2A 4AP

Printed and bound in Portugal

90 0 9 8 7 6 5 4 3 2 1

Photograhic Credits:
Front Cover L. R. Dawson/Bruce Coleman p.4 Liz & Tony Bomford/Ardea p.5 Francisco Erize/Bruce Coleman p.6-7 E. A. James/NHPA p.8 Francois Gohier/Ardea p.9 Dr.
Eckart Pott/Bruce Coleman p.10 Stephen Krasemann/NHPA p.11 Annie Price/Survival Anglia p.12 Francois Gohier/Ardea p.13 Dr. Eckart Pott/Bruce Coleman p.14 Sylvia
Harcourt/Survival Anglia p.15 top Jeff Foott/Survival Anglia bottom B. & C. Alexander p.16 Kim Westerskov p.17 Francois Gohier/Ardea p.18-19 B. & C. Alexander

Illustration Credits:
p.4-19 David Cook/Linden Artists p.20-21 Stephen Lings/Linden Artists p.24-25 Malcolm Livingstone p.26-30 Graeme Corbett p.31 Alan Rogers

CONTENTS

LOOKING AT SEALS

Seals spend most of their lives in water, but surprisingly their closest relatives are land mammals like cats, dogs and bears. Seals have dog-like faces and large, doleful eyes. Their bodies are streamlined and they have flippers rather than legs to help them swim.

Most seals live in large groups called colonies, but some live alone or in smaller groups. Seals can be found in oceans around the world, but are most common in the cooler waters near the North and South Poles.

There are over 30 different kinds of seals, including sea lions and walruses. The seal family is divided into three main groups – true seals, eared seals and walruses.

Like cats and dogs, all seals have whiskers.

Some seals can bend their backs until their heads touch their back flippers.

◀ A grey seal colony at home in the cold North Sea. Seals have a thick layer of fat under their skin called blubber that helps keep them warm in the water. Blubber is also a useful source of energy for the seals when they cannot find food.

▶ Elephant seals are the largest seals in the world. Out of all the animals that live in the sea, only whales are bigger. Fully-grown male elephant seals have long, curved noses rather like elephants' trunks.

TRUE SEALS

True seals are sometimes called earless seals because they have no ear flaps, only small holes. Their back flippers trail behind their bodies close together. Their front flippers are quite short. True seals use their front flippers to help them get out of the water or over small obstacles.

On land true seals move by making an awkward humping movement with their bodies, but in water they travel with speed and grace. To swim, they move the back of their bodies from side to side. Their front flippers are used to change direction or to paddle.

Some of the most interesting members of the seal family are true seals. The huge elephant seals are the largest seals in the world and can

be over five metres (17 feet) long. Weddell seals are champion divers. They can dive to great depths and stay underwater for over 40 minutes. Most seals come up for air every few minutes.

Although most true seals are slow and clumsy on land, some can move surprisingly quickly. Crabeater seals are the fastest seals on land. They push and thrust themselves along almost as fast as most people run.

One of the strangest true seals is the hooded seal which can inflate its nostrils to form a hood over its head. No one knows what this hood is for, but it makes the seal's voice louder than usual when it is inflated.

There are 19 kinds of true seals, including the harbor or common seals shown below. Harbor seals come ashore to have their babies, but courtship and mating take place in the water.

EARED SEALS

Eared seals are so-called because they have small ear flaps. They also have longer and wider flippers than other seals. Eared seals use their front flippers more than their back ones when they are swimming. On land they gallop by turning their back flippers forward and walking on all fours.

The eared seal family includes approximately 14 kinds of sea lions and fur seals. California sea lions are the seals you are most likely to see in zoos and circuses. They learn tricks easily and make star performers. Stellar or northern sea lions are the largest eared seals. They can be as long as tigers.

Fur seals have thicker coats than other seals. They have a layer of coarse hairs on the outside of their bodies and a second, softer coat

SEAL FACTS

On land, fur seals tuck their front flippers under their bodies when they are cold and fan themselves with their back flippers when they are hot!

underneath. Fur seals are hunted for their fur coats, as are several other kinds of seals.

Among the most interesting eared seals are northern fur seals. Female northern fur seals and their young swim over 8000 kilometres (5000 miles) each year. They leave their breeding grounds in Alaska and travel to warmer waters in the south. No one knows why they make this long journey. It takes over six months and during that time the seals never come ashore.

◀ California sea lions live in large groups and often come ashore. They can be seen on Pacific coastlines from British Columbia to Mexico.

▶ Some male fur seals have heavy manes of hair over their heads and necks, like the northern fur seal in this picture. Male northern fur seals are almost twice the size of their mates and can be over four times their weight.

THE WALRUS

Walruses are the only seals that grow tusks. These tusks are really extra-long teeth that can grow up to one metre (39 inches) long. Walruses use their tusks to haul themselves out of the water and, sometimes, to fight.

Walrus families stay together longer than any other seal families. The mother has to stay with her young for nearly two years while their tusks are growing. Walruses are born a dull, brown colour but grow a thin, reddish-brown coat. They can be over three metres (ten feet) long when fully grown.

For over 1000 years walruses were hunted for their ivory tusks and tough skins. Today they are an endangered species and are protected by law.

▼ Walruses can be seen lying closely packed together on northern coastlines.

HOW SEALS TALK

Seals are very talkative and can make a large variety of noises. Sea lions make loud, barking noises. Walruses communicate by bellowing at each other – a sound which can be heard nearly a kilometre (two-thirds of a mile) away.

Male seals can be very aggressive during the breeding season. When two meet, the larger seal may open his mouth and make a quiet hissing sound or utter loud, threatening barks. The smaller seal usually backs off.

▲ These two male elephant seals are challenging each other. If neither backs down, they may snap at each other's heads and shoulders.

SEAL FACTS

When female seals are approached by unwanted males, they roll onto their sides and wave their flippers in the air. This drives the males away!

Mother seals can recognise their babies by their cries and their scent. Nosing is used as a means of identification between them.

ROOKERIES

Every year seals come ashore to mate and have their babies. Some gather together in huge groups called rookeries. Most rookeries are on remote islands where no one lives. Some are on large beaches. There can be as many as 150,000 seals in a rookery.

The male seals, called bulls, come ashore first and fight each other for space on the beach. When the females, or cows, come ashore they team up with the bulls. Some bulls may have as many as 50 cows in their

territory. The cows are already pregnant when they arrive. They give birth to their babies made during their previous year's mating. Then they mate again.

Rookeries stay together for up to two months. The bulls never leave the shore because they have to guard their territory and mate. They lose a lot of weight and may eat sand and pebbles to fill their empty stomachs.

◀ Only the strongest bulls win territory on the beach and have a chance to mate.

▶ This picture shows a northern fur seal rookery. How many bulls can you see? What tells them apart from the other seals?

BORN ASHORE

Baby seals are called pups. Most seal pups are tiny replicas of their parents, but some have beautiful, thick fur coats to keep them warm until they have built up a layer of blubber. These pups are given special names like whitecoats or bluebacks. Seal pup's fur is very valuable and every year many pups are slaughtered by ruthless hunters.

The pups drink their mother's milk at first, like human babies. The milk is rich and fatty and the pups double in weight within weeks of birth. Some cows feed their pups frequently while others leave their young for days at a time. When the cows mate again, their pups are in danger of being squashed.

PUP FACTS

Harbor seal pups can swim from birth and begin diving when they are a few days old.

Seal pups sleep and play together in the rookery while their mothers are away.

Some seal pups begin swimming and moving on land within hours of being born while others are helpless for several days until their muscles develop. It takes grey seal pups about three weeks to grow full coats of fur before they can start to swim.

When the rookeries break up and the adult seals return to the sea, the pups have to learn to fend for themselves.

They must become master swimmers and be able to catch and eat fish. It is a very dangerous time for young pups, especially if they are born on rocky coastlines and have to learn to swim in rough seas.

Seals can live for up to 40 years. Most cows have their first pups when they are about six years old and have one pup every year until they are nearly 20.

▲ Harbor seal pups can be seen swimming with their mothers during the first few weeks of their lives. However, when they stop drinking her milk, they will travel to new areas.

► Harp seal mothers feed their pups for only a few weeks before returning to the sea to mate again. Left alone, the pups must quickly learn how to fend for themselves.

◄ A beautiful Galapagos sea lion mother waits patiently while her cub is feeding. Some mothers feed their cubs for over a year. The Galapagos sea lion colony spends much more time in its breeding ground than is usual. The first cubs are born in May and the last in December.

A FISHY DIET

Not a lot is known about how seals catch their food in the dark depths of the sea. They keep their eyes open, but close up their ears and nostrils. They probably use their whiskers as sensors to detect the fish and other sources of food.

Unlike people, who take deep breaths before they dive, seals breathe out so that their lungs are empty when they are underwater. They take deep breaths when they come up to the surface. While they are underwater seals get air from special stores in their blood system, and their heart beat slows so that they use up the air very slowly.

Seals like to eat all kinds of sea food, including fish, squid, octopus and shellfish.

Elephant seals catch sharks and large fish. Walruses eat the soft bodies of clams and other shellfish. Leopard seals, so-called because of their spotty coats, eat penguins and other seal's pups. Crabeater seals do

▲ Common seals hunt in the icy Arctic waters, resting on ice floes when they are far from the shore.

◀ A New Zealand fur seal moves gracefully through the water looking for its next meal. It will stay underwater for a few minutes before returning to the surface for air.

not eat crabs! They have special teeth which they use to strain tiny creatures out of the water.

Seals have sharp pointed teeth which means they cannot chew their food. When they catch small fish they swallow them whole. If they catch a big meal, they swim to the water's surface and tear off bite-sized pieces of meat.

SWIMMING FACTS

Seals can sleep underwater! Their bodies automatically rise when they need air and then sink below again.

SEALS AND PEOPLE

Seals have few natural enemies. Polar bears eat ringed and harp seals. Whales and sharks may attack seals in the water, but the seals can defend themselves by swimming close to the shore or taking a deep dive. The seal's worst enemy is man.

People have hunted seals for hundreds of years for their meat, fur and blubber. Oils found in seal blubber can be made into soap and other products. Most seal hunters work during the breeding seasons when the seals are on land and have little chance of escape.

Fishermen think seals are a menace and sometimes kill them on sight. They say that seals eat too many fish and damage their fishing nets.

Once-deserted beaches have become busy seaside resorts and the seals that went there to form their rookeries now have nowhere to go.

In 1988 thousands of seals died from a mysterious virus. Some scientists believe that the virus was caused by the huge amounts of waste that we put in the sea.

Conservation groups all over the world are trying to save seals. Several countries have banned the sale of seal skins. Governments are being asked to make some beaches into nature reserves so that all seals have somewhere to mate and have their babies.

You can help seals by joining conservation and wildlife groups and not buying seal fur products.

◀ Inuit people hunt seals to provide food, clothes and other materials for their community, but commercial hunters often kill seal pups for their fur coats alone.

▶ A manmade platform provides these fur seals with a place to rest after swimming in the cold Arctic waters.

OCEAN GAME

Follow the young seal on its journey to the breeding grounds. To play this game you will need a dice and some counters.

BE CAREFUL – if you land on a black square you have to start again.

START

Chased by shark. Forward 4 spaces.

Dive for fish. Miss a turn.

Polluted seas. Throw again.

Rest ashore. Miss a turn.

Chased by elephant seal. Back 3 spaces.

Rough seas. Back 3 spaces.

Rocky coastline. Miss a turn.

Caught in fishing net. Miss a turn.

Take short cut to avoid fishermen.

Walrus gives directions. Forward 3 spaces.

Ride the waves. Forward 2 spaces.

Stop to rest. Miss a turn.

FINISH

SEAL MASK

Try making a mask. You will need a piece of card or thick paper, a length of elastic, string or lace and a pair of scissors.

Draw the basic mask shape on to the card. Remember to make two holes for your eyes and a small hole at each side of the mask. Carefully cut out your mask shape and then decide how you are going to decorate it. When your mask is decorated, thread the elastic, string or lace through the two holes at the side of the mask.

There are lots of ways to decorate masks. Here are a few things to try.

crayons

wool

paint

fabric

coloured paper

◄ Our mask was made by cutting this basic shape from card and covering it with fabric.

FIND THE SEALS

There are six seals hiding in this picture. Can you find them all?

There is one more animal in the picture. Do you know its name?

THE GREAT GATHERING

BY LUCY BAKER

The sea was thick with bodies. Hundreds of male seals were swimming towards their annual mating grounds. When they reached the shoreline, they hauled themselves out of the water and began to move up the sandy beach. As more and more arrived, so the rookery took shape.

To the seabirds circling above, it must have looked as if the bulls were playing an elaborate game. Moving back and forth, they hissed and roared and bellowed at one another. The air was cracked and shaken by their calls. In fact, the bulls were anything but playful. They were competing for territory, an area of the beach that they could control over the coming weeks. There was not enough room for everyone and only the strongest bulls would stay to become this year's beachmasters.

A young bull called Pinniped flapped out of the water and came to rest on the sandy shore. Lifting his head high, he looked about him for an unclaimed section of the rookery. Last year he had got this far but no further. Arriving late, he had been unable to find a single space. He could have tried to take territory from one of the settled bulls, but he had been too small to make the challenge.

This year things were going to be different. Pinniped was ten now and stronger than he had ever been. He would find a space and find it quickly. With a yelp of relief, he saw an opening a short distance up the beach and moved towards it.

As he made his ungainly way, Pinniped noticed that the female seals were beginning to arrive. They stood in clumps while the bulls tried to impress them with aggressive posing and loud calls. Eventually, the cows would form harems around the beachmasters.

Pinniped moved carefully through the rookery to avoid the seals on either side of him. The bulls cast him suspicious looks and, when he got too close, they started to lumber towards him, uttering low, hissing threats. Pinniped hurried on, head down. He did not want to get into a territorial feud. Fights betweeen bull seals look comical but they are really bloody and painful.

At last, Pinniped reached the space he had seen from the shoreline. He made a few loud calls to claim the land as his own, but things were not going to be that easy. A sudden roar caused Pinniped to twist round. Behind him, a terrifyingly large bull was reared for attack.

Pinniped had only a few moments to decide what to do. He could run or he could fight. His challenger already had a large territory nearby where many females were gathering. He did not need more space. Pinniped made up his mind. He was going to hold his ground. He roared defiantly and the sound scattered the nearby gulls.

The challenging bull began to sway and, for a few moments, Pinniped was mesmerised by the movement. Then, with a mighty crash, head struck head. Pinniped's ears began ringing, but he did not budge. Pushing forward, he faced his opponent again.

For a time the fighting continued. Panting and groaning the two bulls butted, pushed and snapped at one another. But age was on Pinniped's side. His challenger, for all his size and might, was old. He did not have the energy to keep up his attack for long. As the older bull felt his strength drain away, he began to back away. From a safe distance, he gave a final roar of disapproval and then lumbered back to his territory.

Young Pinniped swelled with pride. Now he was a true beachmaster. He had won his place in the rookery and no one would take it away from him.

In the following weeks, Pinniped learned much about rookery life. Seven cows joined him in his territory and each gave birth to a small, silky pup a few days after arriving. The pups were weak and helpless at first, but quickly gained strength from their mother's milk. By the time they were a week old, they were left alone for hours at a time, while their mothers went to the sea to hunt.

Mating with the cows in his harem had not been as easy as Pinniped had thought. And the small, delicate pups, always so close to their mothers' sides, made him nervous. He was so much bigger than they were. One careless move and he could squash them flat.

With every passing day, Pinniped's hunger increased. He wished he could leave his territory and go hunting. But although he had won his position in the rookery, not a day went by without a new challenge from one of the nearby bulls. If his back was turned for one moment, his territory could be lost. To calm his rumbling belly, Pinniped swallowed rocks and pebbles that he found on the sand, but they were a poor substitute for fresh fish.

After three weeks ashore and not a bite to eat, Pinniped decided to leave the rookery. He had mated with all seven cows in his harem and his time as beachmaster had come to an end. Reaching the water's edge, he looked back at the growing pups basking in the sunshine. It would be some time before they took the plunge and left the safety of the beach.

He would miss life at the rookery. He would miss being a beachmaster. But next year he would return again and, somewhere close by, seven of his own offspring would start their lives.

TRUE OR FALSE ?

Which of these facts are true and which ones are false? If you have read this book carefully, you will know the answers.

1. Seals have whiskers, like cats and dogs.
2. Walruses are the only seals with tusks.
3. True seals have large ear flaps.
4. Seals are faster on land than in water.

5. Fur seals tuck their flippers under their bodies when they are cold.
6. Seal bulls may eat sand and pebbles during the mating season.

7. Seals take deep breaths before diving underwater.
8. Seals can sleep underwater.

9. Weddell seals can stay underwater for over 40 minutes.
10. Sea lions are the seals you are most likely to see in zoos and circuses.
11. Elephant seals are the smallest seals in the world.
12. Seal pups have no fur on their bodies.
13. Most seals live in tropical waters.

14. Seals can live for over 100 years.
15. Inuits hunt seals to provide food and clothing for their community.